A Journey IN THE AIR

SAVORN M. YANG

outskirts
press

"Journey In The Air" is about life and living. This flock of wild ducks has a difficult time searching for food in the summer. The food source is very hard to find when the water is dried up in ponds. Far in a great distance, they have to go because life could not be any better without food. But, what else could be the problem when food is not easy to find. Please, enjoy the story.

Contents

In A Hot Summer Day

IN A NEW dawn of the day, the sun tries to break its way across the sky as it usually does. It is very early in the morning in the middle of hot summer. The drops of morning dew are still holding onto the very tips of grass and bushes. At the beginning of the day, the cool breeze rushes across the atmosphere and it is nice and cool in the morning. It seems like the wind tries to dry the drops of dew from the tips of grass and bushes. But, it does not work because the sun is still very much buried in the thick clouds of the morning. Of course, it is beautiful day and birds are already up flying from tree to tree to find food. Others are still staying in the bushes and hopping from branch to branch as they wish.

All of sudden, there is a huge cloud of tiny insects coming from nowhere and this huge cloud of insects drifts just about a few feet above the bushes. These tiny insects try to fly against the wind aimlessly in the opened space above the grassy field. Up in the opened space, they seem very much to compete against one another to go ahead, flying against the flow of the wind. This is not looking good as they rush against the current of the wind. They are so small and don't have the strength to keep themselves floating in the air. Unfortunately, there is a small number of insects dropping down on the grass because they have broken wings. The little insects struggle to crawl through a thick jungle of tall grass to find their way to safety. Now, their lives would dramatically change for the worst because they are no longer flying away to safety.

Others continue flying as far as they can. Some of them seem to get carried away by the wind. The thick cloud of these tiny insects rush over the bushes by a strong push of the cool breeze in the morning. Once again, some others try their best to get over the bushes and they just can't do it, not because they do not know how to fly, but because they fly close to the bushes. Then, they get blown into the bushes and their little transparent wings get sticked in the drops of morning dew. They try very hard kicking, and moving their bodies back and forth to pull their wings from the morning dew. These little insects struggle to break free from the morning dew, but there is no use. After a long struggling to get free, there are some of the little insects breaking their wings and they fall to the ground.

Now, the sun breaks through the thick clouds and it shines bright on the atmosphere. Also, the sun shines through gaps between branches. There are so many little insects flying toward that bright sunlight and they are exactly just like a fine dust drifting in the air. Wherever the sunlight shines through the bushes, there is a cloudy spot of insects drifting in that bright light. They seem to enjoy the warm of the sunlight and they just can't fly away from the sunlight.

Since it is bright and a fabulous day. There are other, big and small, creatures coming out for the sunlight in the morning. They have been peacefully sleeping all night long. Now, it is certainly the time for them to get up and ready for a new day. Long resting over night, these creatures wake up in the morning hungry. Most of them travel a great distance to look for their food and some of them do not need to go far searching for their food. For instance, at this site, small birds that are busy hopping from branches to branches look at insects crawling in the grass. Then, they come down quickly from branches and hop on the grass to investigate. For sure enough, they know exactly what they are looking for. The little birds come to peck insects one by one to eat. That would not take long and others (frogs, lizards, and crickets) come to the site in order to have some insects to eat. Also, there are some birds flying above the bushes and they just swoop up and down to peck the insect in the air while they are flying circles in the sunlight.

This has been a wild feeding ground and the hungry creatures can eat as much as they want and they quickly disappear in the bushes and in tall grass. Once again, the sun makes its way for the high noon and the heat begins heating in the atmosphere. It is very hot and calm. Gradually, the temperature of the day is slowly changed as the time goes by. There is no cool breeze in the afternoon. Other small birds stay in cool shade under the bushes and some other big birds stay up in tall trees. Some other creatures bury themselves in the sand under bushes so that they will not get burned in the heat of the sun. Frogs jump in water to get themselves to cool down. This is the hottest part of the day in the afternoon.

As the day gets blasted by the heat from the sun, a flock of wild ducks has to come to a pond to cool themselves and perhaps to get something to eat as well. When they are in the pond, these wild ducks make loud noises. They flap their wings and dip their bodies in the deep water to get cooled down while they are in the water. Others submerge deeper in the water searching for small fish to eat. This is not a good day for little fish, fresh water shrimp and other small lives living in the pond. They are frantically very scared and swimming fast around circles in the pond to get away from hungry ducks. They try to keep themselves at a distance and also try not to be caught by aggressive beaks of wild ducks.

Unfortunately, little fish, shrimp and other small lives have very little chances to beat the odds that stark against their lives. First, it is in the middle of summer and it is very hot. Secondly, the water in the pond is obviously very low and it has literally no rain for almost two months. This is a severe punishment from nature which is badly hurting those little lives living in a shallow water. And at last, there are many wild ducks staying in the water. They are here, not only to get themselves to cool down in the pond, but they also have to find something to eat. The hungry ducks spread themselves all over the pond to catch some small fish, shrimp and other species that live in bottom of the pond.

In other words, chances are very slim to survive in a pond with shallow water. This is because of the extreme heat in the summer and the rain does not come very often in a dry season. The water could possibly go lower at this time of the year. On the other hand, wild ducks have more advantages to catch their food. They use their feet and beaks to stir up in every part of the pond and the water becomes cloudy. The pond looks big and roomy and perhaps fish and other species could probably escape death, but hungry ducks have already scattered themselves to different parts of the pond and waited for the fish to make a move. This is very difficult to get away from starved ducks. Of course, every turn that a small school of fish tries hard to get away from the ducks is impossible. There are some fishes caught in the beaks of hungry ducks and others have to jump about several inches above the surface of water in order to escape the aggressive beaks of hungry wild ducks.

This is certainly one of the corners where the pond is stretching a little further underneath the overgrown bushes. This is the spot in which is literally kept cool all summer long. On the other side of the overgrown bushes is a big hill made by ants for years. The sunlight is hardly getting through these thick bushes. At the moment, there are no birds, frogs and small animals staying around here because they are scared to be around at the present of wild ducks. Little tropical birds fly away, cricket crawl back in the holes underneath the thick grass where they keep themselves in the summer and frogs quickly jump in the water. All trees, bushes and other wild plants around here stay green because there is plenty of water for them to grow bigger and taller. Deep down in the pond, there are many big and small roots stretching far to the bottom of the pond.

Once again, this is the safe place in the pond. Most species that live in the bottom of the pond come to this spot because the wild ducks would not catch anything because there are many roots. And behind these roots, there are several tiny holes where small fish, shrimp and other small species can safely hide from hungry wild ducks. This is a quiet moment and the water become cloudy because a flock ducks badly stir up the mud in the bottom of the pond. They do not make as much as noises when they got here. The ducks stay floated in the water looking around. Some of them run their beaks on their backs and wings. Others stretch their necks longer and flap their wings hard to sake of water from feathers and a few of them swim around circle, just to keep themselves busy.

Then, there are two young ducks slowly swimming away from the flock. They seem to be curious even though they have been here in this pond for several times in the previous years. In just a few minutes, the two young ducks make a left turn and quietly swim straight to the overgrown bushes that hung over a corner of the pond. In this part of the pond is much different from the other parts. It has more shade and it is a cool spot to stay away from the heat of the sun. A few feet above the water, there are many small branches hanging down to water and there are also many stings of vines growing and wrapping around the branches. Obviously, it looks just like cave to stare up from the lower water in the pond.

The two young ducks come into this place and they do not want to waste anytime. They submerge to the bottom of the pond to search for something to eat. At same moment, a small school of fish and other species quickly rush into deep little holes behind roots. They chase big fish around the corner, but they do not catch them. Instead, they can only catch little fishes because small fishes do not swim fast enough to get away from the wild ducks. Then, they both come to the surface of the water to catch some breath. They quickly flap their wings and swim circle around for a couple of times to see if there is anything strength coming up for them.

For the second time, they try again submerging to the bottom of the pond. This time, there is nothing found, not even a small fish to catch. One of them begin running his beak in the soft mud and a long the roots and hopes that he will catch something. For a while, he keeps trying to run his beak in the soft mud and also running beak a long the roots. Still, he does not catch anything. He comes up to the surface to catch some breath. He quickly looks around and does not see his buddy come up to the surface, yet. Then, he quickly gets back down to the bottom of the pond and focuses on catching fish or something to eat. This time, he starts on the other side of the pond and begins running his beak along the roots. It is soon enough he grabs on something big and soft.. He tries to yank this big fish and brings it to the surface so that he can swallow it. Obviously, he can not swallow anything while he is under the water.

However, this is a very surprise for him and he does not expect this to happen. As he keeps trying to pull this big fish, something else smacks him hard in the face. Quickly, he lets go the big fish and he come up to the surface with fear for his life. While he is floating in the surface of the water, he looks around to see if his flock is still here in the pond. He seems to be lost, or confused. Literally, he swims alone by himself looking for his buddy. Because of the smack in his face, he seems not to be himself. He was very scared when he got hit in the face while he was under the water. All of sudden, he is about to swim to his flock and he accidentally catches a big frog sitting quietly on dry land in a corner of his right eye. Of course, the young duck does not look all right, but he tries to be normal as much as he can try. Obviously, in the eyes of a big frog, he is far from normal.

"Hey, little duck. Are you okay?", asks Mr. Big Frog.

"No, I did not know what it was hitting me in the face", said the little duck.

"What happened?", asked Mr. Big Frog. "I think I pecked on a big fish and suddenly I got whacked in my face. There is something strange down there in the bottom of the pond", said the little duck.

"Are you scared?", asked Mr. Big Frog. "Yes, I am. I still did not know what hit me", said the little duck.

"Are you by yourself?", asked Mr. Big Frog.

"No, I am here with my buddy and my flock is still here on the side of the pond", said the little duck. Now, the big frog know who was grabbing and pulling his hind leg while he was hiding under the water, but he does not want to say anything about the duck getting hit in the face. Of course, Mr. Big Frog pretends not to know anything. He was just toying with the little duck.

At this huge pond, the big frog has been here for little over fifteen years. He has seen it all good and bad events taken place in this pond. It seems to be true that big and strong characters would be dominant in the wilderness. The big guy would aggressively stand up to fight for his place and respects others. Once again, this big guy has more chances to live longer than the rest. For example, the big frog has learned a lot about life surviving in this great danger and the skills to protect himself. However, the wilderness is obviously a vicious place where small and vulnerable species can not protect themselves. They have very less chances to survive on their own. There is always a danger existed in the surrounding area for almost every minute and these young and innocent lives are often lost to aggressive predictors.

Mr. Big Frog is not considered big, but for himself comparing to other frogs, he is a big frog. The frog. Of course, he could possibly be picked up and eaten by foxes and wild cats if he does not pay attention to surrounding area where he lives. The big frog has well done it all to live this long. Master his surviving skills, he has stood up against all odds. He knows what to do when trouble comes. Water and soft mud are the weapon used to hide himself from dangerous animals. Perhaps, this big frog has faced the fear and fought for his life. Days and nights, he never puts down his guard for one minute.

For a while, as the little duck has a conversation with the frog, his buddy popped up the surface to catch his breath and has his wing flapped very fast to sake the water of his feather. Then, the two young ducks swim circle facing each other. They both start having a conversation and the frog stays quietly on dry land and watches them talking to each other and of course the frog would not have any idea what these two young ducks talking about. The two ducks sway to the left and then to the right and the conversation seems not to have an ending. The tone of their conversation gets louder, sometimes and other times it sounds reasonably, not screaming back and forth.

This has been for a while and they seem not to let go, whatever was the problem that these two young ducks have. Then, the frog decides to cut in their conversation and finds out why these two are not literally at the same page. The frog moves slowly close to the water and he tightens his stomach. " The two ducks quickly turn around and look at the frog sitting by the water. That was really a very quiet moment and no body is talking. After that, the young ducks swim straight to the shore where the frog is calmly sitting.

"What was that!" ,asked the gray duck. " Nothing, but I just don't like the tone that you talk to each other", said Mr. Frog. "Are we that bad yelling at each other?", said the spotty duck.

"May be I don't understand what you have talk to each other, but the look on your faces tell me something wrong between you two", said Mr. Frog.

"We are just talking", said the gray duck. "I look old to you, but I am too old and deaf", said Mr. Frog.

"Sorry, Mr frog. We have something that needs to be clear", said the spotty duck.

"I know I should not get involved intothis, but I don't want to see you two doing something that make you feel regret later", said Mr. Frog.

"No, we don't any bad thing to each other", said the gray duck.

"The funny is that I can't imagine to see you two getting big. I remember the day when you came here with yous folks and you were very small", said Mr. Frog.

"You better believe that. I've been here longer than your folks. I've lost many good friends of mine in this pond. There are also many sad stories buried in my head. I have to live them until my time comes", said Mr. Frog.

"Have you ever been any where beside this pond?" , asked the spotty duck.

"No, I've been here all my life. I wish I could go away from this pond. I don't mean that this is a bad place to live. In this my birth place, I have many bad memories and I feel depressed when I think about my friends and folks", said Mr. Frog.

"Mr. frog, we are so sorry to hear your story, especially about your friends and family who have their cut short", said the spotty duck.

"That is okay, I appreciate that. May be someday I would find a way to get out of here and I would start a new life", said the frog.

"Mr. frog, we would help you find a way to get out of here", said the spotty duck. This was no warning and the spotty duck gets smacked behind the back of his head and he quickly turns to look at the gray duck and says,, " what was that for." The gray duck stares at the spotty duck and gives him a little smile and says, " It is time to go." The gray duck does not want to say anything to spotty duck, yet. He waits patiently until they leave Mr. frog. In the moment, the gray duck does not want to say anything because Mr. frog might get upset. On the other hand, the spotty duck does not realize what he have himself got into. He acts like everything can get done at the tip of his tongue. He never thinks hard enough before he opens his mouth.

Then, the gray duck has to cut in the conversation between Mr. Frog and the spotty duck and says, " I am sorry Mr. Frog. It is time for us to go and I am sure we will see you again at the place." Quickly, the big Frog turns to look at the gray duck and says, "you two have a good day and it is to talk to you both." " Thank you Mr. Frog", said the gray duck. It is about a few seconds turning around and swimming back to their flock and the spotty duck turns to the big frog and says," we would help you find a way to a new place." The big frog stands still alone looking at the two young ducks swimming back to their parents. Nothing else to do in the afternoon, the frog takes a rest.

It is about half way back to the flock and there is no warning again. The spotty duck does not expect anything to happen. Then, he gets smacked behind the back of hie head and he just had it and he pushes the gray duck as hard as he could. And the tone of his voice is expressed in an unpleasant mood. The spotty duck says, "What is wrong with you. Say something and I can hear you. I literally don't like getting hit in the back of my head. Again, if you have a problem, talk to me and let me know what is in your head." It was a silent moment and at the same time the gray duck stared at the spotty duck and it is kind of silent treatment. The spotty duck says, " Do I look funny to you? What is wrong with me and you just dress me with your eyes in a funny way. Are you going to hit me again? I just don't understand why you are acting this way."

Literally, the gray duck just stays still and does not move an inch with his eyes looking at the spotty duck. He just can't believe what the spotty duck has said to Mr. frog without realizing the condition of the day. It is extremely hot in the summer and the hot air is blown across the atmosphere and the spotty duck wants to help Mr. frog to find a new place. Obviously, traveling a long distance in this kind of weather is very dangerous and it would possibly cause life and death, especially Mr. frog travels on foot. He would not have a chance to make through the extreme heat of the day. Plus, there are many other dangerous animals scattering all over places looking for food to eat. With this kind of violence which is waiting to happen down the road, it is very impossible to find a new place for Mr. frog. This is the reason why the gray duck does not like hearing what the spotty duck has talked to Mr. frog about searching a new pond.

"Yes, you look funny and stupid and you think that in your own world is perfect and everything else is just fine", said the gray duck.

"What are you talking about?", asked the spotty duck.

"Oh! You play innocent. Why you forget so soon? Let me remind you this so that you would know what I'm talking about "We would help you find a new pond", said the gray duck.

"I don't think that there is nothing wrong just to help him to get a new place and we can do that", said the spotty duck.

"First of all, there is no WE getting involved in searching for a new place for Mr. Frog. Secondly, you are not working hard enough with your head and last you are just a little kid", said the gray duck.

"Wait a minute, you don't want to help", said the spotty duck.

"Not this kind of help and I don't want to get involved", said the gray duck.

"Why! I already told Mr. frog that we would do this and now you tell me that you don't want to help", said the spotty duck.

"Whatever you have discussed with Mr. frog, I don't know. The problem is that you don't look and learn. Everything is literally begun with your loud mouth and you don't think before opening your mouth", said the gray duck.

"Wait and wait a minute, this is killing me. you think that I can't see what is happening. At least, I know that Mr. frog needs our help to find a new pond", said the spotty duck.

"Oh my God, you are so stupid. I don't mean that you are blind. What I'm trying to say is that you need to look at things from different angles before you open your mouth", said the gray duck.

"So, this is a reason that you don't want to help Mr. frog", said the spotty duck.

"Helping someone is not my problem, but not knowing how to help someone is irritating me", said the gray duck.

"I don't know what you mean" said the spotty duck.

"Shut up and go home. Everybody starts leaving the pond", said the gray duck.

"Sometimes, I find it hard to follow you", said the spotty duck.

"I'm not talking anymore", said the gray duck.

It is late the evening and the cool breeze just kicks it in and the tips of tall grass and small branches begin rocking back and forth in the wind. Then, there are small birds coming out from bushes and they look for something to eat before the night falls. These small birds hop from branches to other branches and some of them peck something from the ground to eat.

Back in the pond, the flock of wild ducks is still swimming and others flap their wings and get ready to take off. Soon they come together, the leader flaps his wings to pull himself in the air. After that, one by one starts doing the same thing, flapping his or her wings to take off from the surface of calm water. This is actually the sun, once again, buried behind thick clouds, but the bright of yellow and orange trying in the sky from the West. The wind blow a little stronger and tall trees and long limbs begin to sway from side to side. This is a cool part of the day when the sun drifts on its way down to the West and the cool breeze changes the mood of the atmosphere. Of course, all living creatures enjoy the evening and the cool night when they go pleasantly to sleep.

Flying Back Home

IT IS FAR above the surface of the earth and it is very much different from whatever is seen, or looked on the ground. Up in the sky, there is nothing to hold onto. This is a huge opened space in the Universe. The wind and the sky are forever stretching far beyond the eyesight. It is impossible to see the other side of the world as these wild ducks are traveling high in the sky. For traveling up high in the sky, these wild ducks have no problem. They were born to fly naturally like other big birds. They know how to float in the air as long as they can. Since it has been too hot in the summer, most ponds are very much dried up and food is not easy to find. These wild ducks have to travel for hundred of miles to search for their food.

It is now the time to fly back home in the evening. The ducks fly West in the bright red of the sunset. It looks like they are flying toward a burning sky. A quick glance from behind, they look very much like a big flock of crows toward the end of the world. Again, it has been a long day that this huge family of ducks has to go from pond to pond to catch their food. This huge family always travels together as a big group. The leader is also taking the lead to wherever they want to go to look for something to eat. Up in the opened space above the earth, they actually know the route to get home. Day after day, this duck family is busy searching where the food can easily be found so that the members would have something to eat.

Up in the sky, they fly in small groups of four, or six. Sometimes, flying in formation can be a long line of ten to fifteen ducks. They never try to go faster than the leader of the flock. They always follow one another until reaching a destination. For that good behavior, it seems literally that these ducks have been trained to cooperate one another.

Quietly, they keep flying west in small groups. Then, the bright red of the sunset gets dimer and dimer in the West and the strong wind keeps blowing more cool air. This means that the darkness of the night would soon cover up the Universe. Certainly, it does not matter if it gets dark. These wild ducks would still find their way home. They have been flying all their lives in and out on this route and they never get lost. They know well the directions to go around this large area.

Flying in a cool breeze, the two ducks, gray and spotty, stay side by side pretending nothing happened. None of the other ducks knew what has really happened in the pond because they were busy chasing a school of fish in the water. At the moment, the spotty duck takes a quick glance at the gray duck and says nothing to gray duck. The spotty duck can not put the idea of finding a new pond for Mr. frog to rest. Somewhere in the back of his mind, the spotty duck keeps worrying of what to do. Quickly, he looks at the gray duck again and wants to ask him for help. On the other hand, he already knew that the gray duck is not interested in the idea of helping Mr. frog. This idea is quite bothering because he has no other ideas to help Mr. frog.

This for the third times, the spotty duck takes a quick look at the gray duck because he wants to him for some ideas. This time, he does not care what the gray duck is trying to tell him, or to blame him. He just wants to hear what else can the gray duck tells him.

"Hey, you want to talk. It's been quiet for a while", said the spotty duck.

"What you have in mind", said the gray duck.

"You know we've been talking about this subject a while back before we took off from the pond where we met Mr. frog", said the spotty duck.

"What subject or it is a new subject", said the gray duck.

"Well, it is about a way to help Mr. frog", said the spotty duck.

"Oh, no. I told you already that I don't want to get involved ", said the gray duck.

"Why? I don't want to see Mr. frog suffering because that would dry up soon and then he would die", said sadly the spotty duck.

"Look, to find a new pond for Mr. frog is simply easy, but to take him there is very dangerous and would die on the way to get there", said the gray duck.

Soon the word DIE comes out from the gray duck's beak, it is a long pause and the spotty duck seems to lose his words. He is quiet for the moment and starts thinking for the reason why the gray duck said that Mr. frog could die on the way to a new pond. In the back of his mind, the spotty duck does not like the sound of what the gray duck has said. He would think that the gray duck does want to help. Also, the spotty duck keeps thinking that the gray duck was trying to scare him. The spotty duck does not like what the gray duck has said horrible thing would happen to Mr. Frog. Then, he speeds up to catch up with the gray duck and he wants to question how a bad thing would surely happen to Mr. Frog by trying to help him to get to a new place.

"Look, I understood what you've said, but how you would know all of this could happen to Mr. Frog", said the spotty.

"What! Are you seriously to do that, helping Mr. Frog?", said the gray duck.

"That is the reason why I ask for your help", said the spotty duck.

"I have completely nothing against Mr. frog, but I can see that there is nothing that I can do to help him. Sorry that I have to say this way. I tell you the truth", said the gray duck.

"I just can't see the reason why you don't want to give a try. I don't think it is going to hurt you if you give a try", said the spotty duck.

"My goodness, you awfully ask for a lot of troubles and they will definitely hurt you badly. When it comes to that point, you can not forgive yourself because of a stupidity you make in your life", said the gray duck.

"At least, I try to ask you for help and I try hard and you still say no. I want me to beg you with belly lying flat on the ground", said the spotty duck.

"I try to explain you the reason why I can't help and you just can't see my point. I wish I could open your two eyes so that you can see clearly what I am trying to tell you", said the gray duck.

Quickly, the gray duck turns away from the spotty duck and he knows that the spotty duck will not take NO for an answer. The gray duck knows that it is no use to keep explain the bad consequences which would exist in a way that the spotty duck wants to help Mr. frog to a new pond. All of sudden, he just dives straight toward the earth because he finally gets home. The other ducks fly circle to get lower and lower and then they glide to the ground.

On the ground, it is getting dark and the cool wind gently blows across the atmosphere. there is a huge sandy field with small bushes here and there by a lake. There are also other flocks of birds, like swans and Snow gooses, sharing the same spot with wild duck family. The moment of their arrival, other big birds are resting on the sand stand up and look around to see who are coming in at this late of the day. All the birds walk around and make noises for a few minutes and then they are all quietly going back to sleep again. Through the night, some birds sleep with their bellies lying flat to the cool sand and others sleep standing on their feet.

Finally, everybody rests peacefully in the night with the cool breeze brushing gently on their feather. Night time is a pleasant part of the day because almost every moment of living thing has come to rest in a favorite spot. it does not matter where is a favorite place located in the water, on dry land,or up in a tall tree. These big birds need plenty of resting at night because they travel literally for hundred and hundred of miles in day time to search for food. Every day, these big birds are very busy searching for what they can eat, just trying to survive from day to day.

This is much deeper into the cool night and the wind keeps rushing the cool breeze through the atmosphere. Most exhausted ducks are comfortably resting, but one of them seems to be staying awake. He has his belly down to the soft sand and his wings cover the entire body. Sometimes, he has his head buried in his right wing. Other times, he has neck stretched a bit longer and turned from side to side. Once in a while, he runs his beak down to his belly and underneath of his wings. Then, he stands up and flaps his wings. He just stands still looking around for a few second in his own curiosity in the dark of the night. After that, he lows his body to the soft sand and goes back to sleep.

Obviously, this is not a good night resting for this poor little duck. Of course, there is something bothering that little duck. He can not stay still and goes to sleep. Again, he stands up and takes a few steps walking toward another duck sleeping by a thin bush. He stretches his right wing to push the sleeping gently. The sleeping duck wakes up and quickly looks around. Of course, it is still dark and he looks at the duck standing by him.

"What are you doing? It is still dark and I'm sleeping", said the gray duck.

"I can't sleep", said the spotty duck.

"It is in the middle of the night and I don't want to talk", said the gray duck.

"Can we stop by the pond to see Mr. Frog?", asked the spotty duck.

"Are you out of your mind? First, I don't have anything to do with Mr. Frog and secondly, I'm trying to get some sleep", said the gray duck.

"I desperately need your help", said the spotty duck.

"Are you kidding me!", said the gray duck.

Then, a deep voice comes from the crowd and says, " we all try to get some sleep." The two of them can not tell where the voice comes from and the spotty duck lows himself to the ground and the two of them stop talking. Again, the two of them sleep side by side through the night.

The spotty duck is the younger in the flock. He has a good heart and a feeling of taking care for elderly. He was born to a caring duck family and he is taught to respect and to be helpful for others. He always sees the world is a peaceful place to live and everything else is easy to get. Under the care of his parents, spotty duck has his own vision in a way of loving and care for one another. On the other hand, he does not realize, just yet, how bad the real world is and how difficult life is to live from one day to the next. Also, he does not quite understand how hard to be living through each day in the real world. Of course, surviving in this world is to search for hope and prosperity and beside that life is not getting any better. He is too young to make his own decision and he will have a lot to learn in his life time. Now, he sees only the good aspect of life which is well fitting in the expectation of society. These are the guidelines which his parents want him to follow and to be good. This young duck listens well to his parents and he is literally trying to do the right thing for the others.

The orange light starts to brighten up in the East and the darkness begins slowly to fade away. The cool wind still blows across the lake and rushes through the field where flocks of wild duck resting for the night. The tips of small branches in the bushes gradually begin to rock back and forth under the breeze of the morning wind. Early in the morning, there are some small tropical birds hopping from branches to branches to look around the area. They seem to be curios when they wake up early in the morning. A few of them keep turning their heads from left to right and start chirping to one another.

Down to the ground, there are many wild ducks and swans just waking up and they make so much noises. Most of them walk around the place and peck each other on the beaks. Then, female ducks and swans take their children to the lake near by and let the little ones swim for the fun of it in the morning. After that, the adult birds flap the wings and walk toward the lake. There are so many of them swimming in the lake and others run their beaks in water trying to catch something to eat. Soon these birds open their eyes early in the morning, they begin to work until the sunset. Literally, these big birds fly in a great distance to search for food, not just for themselves, but also for the family members, as well. They are quite busy day after day trying to look out for their families.

Once again, it is quite a beautiful day. The sun is up and shining bright and the sky is blue with a few white clouds drifting across the opened space. The cool breeze in the morning is still blowing gently through the atmosphere. After a while, a flock of white swans starts to take off from the lake, one by one, flying up in the air. These huge birds flap their wings hard in order to pull their bodies up from the water and fly up higher in the sky. Soon the swans have left the lake, the wild ducks begin taking off and go on their way to find something to eat. Finally, the place is quiet and no one is left behind. On the ground, there are some black and white feathers pushed around in the sand by the current of the wind.

Somewhere up in the sky, the flock of wild ducks are flying across the opened space and they seem not to know where they are supposed to be, but keep flying until they find a good place to look for their food. Obviously, it is hard to find a decent place to catch their meal because most lakes and ponds are dried up in the hot summer season. They have to fly much further in order to find something to catch for meal. At the moment, most of the ducks worry about where they can find a place to catch their meal, but the spotty duck has his own concern about the elderly frog that he met yesterday. He seems to care so much about this elderly frog. On the way to find food with his parents, spotty duck wants to talk to the gray duck, but he holds back because he does not want his parents to know what he is trying to do. He just stays quiet and flies side by side, but he often turns to look at the gray duck. Inside of him, he wants desperately to talk to the gray duck.

Paradise

IT IS ABOUT two hours flying and the flock of wild ducks comes to a huge lake. The body of water in that lake spreads out for almost a mile. There are different water plants spreading out and growing on top of each other. Also, there are several clusters of water grass in the lake here and there. They are standing tall about a couple of feet above the surface of water. On the other side of the lake,there are more water plants like; water lilies, Cardinal Flower, Giant Snow Flakes and Lavender Lady floating on the surface of water.

A long the shoreline, there are some tall trees standing a few feet from each other. These huge trees have big limbs stretching over the water. These huge trees are also the homes of many tropical birds and there are many bird nests built in the trees to keep baby birds safe. On the other side of the lake, there are two big hill standing up like small mountain. There are some thick bushes growing around the hills. Next to the hills, there is a huge cluster of bamboo plants stretching up to the sky.

Behind the two hills, there is a huge field covered in green grass. This is a flat land where most tropical birds come to sunbathing and peck some earth worm for food. However, there no trees or other plants growing in the middle of this field. Again, this flat land is often under water during rainy season. In the summer, this part of the lake is becoming a dried land and many birds, big and small, come here to enjoy themselves.

The flock of wild ducks fly circle over the lake and then one by one comes down to the cool fresh water. Most of them float circle in the water and others quickly dip their heads in the water and flap their wings for joy. They begun to make noises and chase one another for fun. After that, they all spread out to different area to look for something to eat. A few ducks swim by water plants and peck something from green leaves to eat. This is just the right time and the sun has made its way close to noon time. All kinds of birds and other species are quite busy searching for their food sources. There are some birds in the trees swooping down to peck insects from the water plants. Also, there are a few big cranes walking a long the shore with their babies looking for something to feed their children. The big cranes walk ahead of their children so that they can spot small fish swimming in a shallow water or tiny frogs hopping in front of them.

Much further in the lake, there is a small flock of water birds also looking for something to eat. These birds are not big and they have skinny long legs. They can fly about two feet above the water plants. In the warm sun, they are scattering all over the water plants while the wind blows across the lake. Day by day, all these birds and others are very much busy to find food to feed themselves.

Then, there are a few ducks coming up to the surface of water with fish in their mouths. For a short time, they stay floated in the water with their heads up straight to shake the fish go down their throats. They have to catch more fish to feed themselves while they can in the day time. The other ducks do just that trying to catch more fishes to feed themselves. In the evening, they have to fly back home. This is a chance that they have to catch as many fishes as they can.

In the moment, the two ducks, Spotty and Gray pop up to the surface with fishes in their mouths. They quickly lift their heads up straight and shake the fishes to go down the throat. They both swim around to get fresh air for a few minutes and get back down to the bottom of the lake. There are more fishes swimming in the depth of water. Then, the two young ducks look at each other and ready to go down, but Spotty quickly stops Gray for a reason and he really wants to say something to him before going back down to the bottom of the lake. Gray stay floated with his eyes looking Spotty. Again, he is so wondering what Spotty has in his mind and why he needs to tell him, right now. This is a good time to catch and there are plenty of fishes down the bottom of the lake.

"What you have in mind and let my hear it", said the gray duck.

"I really want to go to visit Mr. frog and I'm kind of thinking that you would come a long with me", said the spotty duck.

"You get to be crazy. I just don't understand why I can't open your eye and look around. You just keep asking for more troubles", said the gray duck.

"Why you say that?", asked the spotty duck.

"I'm not obviously pretending to ignore what you plan to do for Mr. Frog. It is none of my business, but you have to know what you are doing because the consequences you will face", said the gray duck.

"So, you don't want to come a long with me", said the spotty duck.

"You already know the answer", said the gray duck.

"Well, it won't take me long and I'll be back", said the spotty duck. After a small conversation with the gray duck, Spotty quickly stretches his wings and flap them very hard and fast enough to pull his body from the lake. Momentarily, the spotty duck's body glides in the air and flies up straight in the sky. Alone, he is flying across blue sky to see his friend, Mr. Frog. Again, the spotty duck seems not to think twice and he sets to do something and he just does it. He does not sit around and begs the gray duck to come a long with him.

Back in the cool lake, the gray duck seems to feel bad and self-fished because he should not let spotty travel by himself. He knows that he has been lately hard on spotty. Also, he knows that he has been acting like a parent trying to have spotty looked into troubles that are not appeared in a bright daylight. This has to do literally with common senses and he knows that he should take time to explain Spotty about the troubles will exist after the actions is slightly done wrong. There are many mistakes about to happen when actions are not literally well considerate in advantage. The gray duck knows quite well that Spotty does not think of whatever he wants to do. That is the reason the gray duck is worrying that Spotty will have to face his own problems because he is very young in the family. Of course, Spotty will have a lot to learn about life.

Again, Gray keeps himself floating around in the water with his mind thinking about Spotty 's well being and his safety. Gray tries to look out for Spotty as he is his own brother. On the other times, he is really frustrated that Spotty seems not to listen to what he tries to tell him. He tries to help Spotty to stay in the right track and at the same time he feels like that Spotty does not need his help. Well, Gray was once a young boy and he remember well his childhood life. Of course, he has awfully made many mistakes in his young life. He still feels very bad, but there is nothing that he can obviously do to change it. Whatever has been done in his early time is a life lesson. For real, this is not a good way to live in a miserable feeling from that terrible experiences. Worrying about what might have happened to Spotty, he decides to go after Spotty.

Up high in the bright sky, Spotty flies fast through thin air like an arrow speeding through white clouds and gliding in the air like a speed of lighting. Of course, he would not slowdown for anything. He has to be in a hurry so that he can be back with his flock. This is just a short visit and he wants to stop by and says hello to Mr. Frog. On his way to see Mr. Frog, it is very quiet, but the noise of the wind blows strongly against his hears and he does not care about that. It is just a normal sound for him because he has heard this noise many times in his life. there are no any bird flying cross his path. Obviously, this is exactly what Gray has describes Spotty as a young male duck. He never stops and thinks of anything; especially danger which can easily hurt or kill him. Spotty looks at the world just like the way he looks at the reflection of the sky in the water. In the back of his mind, Spotty simply thinks that the world is at peace and nothing could go wrong.

This is a very bad idea and the thought of everything is just fine. This is an idea which is a misinterpretation by youngsters about the world is safe. For example, Spotty is one of them and of course he is completely deceived by a quietness in the surrounding area because there is no harm done to anyone, just yet. This way of thinking could easily put life in a dangerous zone. Most youngsters have no life experiences in the world where they are living with their parents and friends. They obviously go along with the crowd and think that life is safe in this peaceful world. They have no idea about the world in which they are living. Some youngster never make to adulthood. The world has gradually changed for the worst. Again, Spotty never thinks of his own actions. He does whatever he wants and never think of the consequences. This youngster has a lot to learn for his own life.

After a short flying in the sky, Spotty flies circle over the pond where Mr. Frog is staying. He quickly lows himself down to the pond. Soon he touches the water, other small frogs jump in the water to keep themselves safe and they want nothing to do with the spotty duck. These little frogs always take precaution and very often look out for themselves. Spotty seems not to pay to little Frogs jumping into the water. He just swims around and flaps its wings. Then, he runs his beak on his back and shakes its feathers while he keeps himself floating circle in the pond. At the same time, Mr. Frog take a look far across the pond to see who is coming. Of course, it is really safe enough to come close to the water and he sees the young duck swimming alone from side to side of the pond. Mr. Frog says " Are you here by yourself." Spotty looks up surprisingly to see Mr. Frog sitting on dry land and he quickly approaches Mr. Frog with a smile on his face. Of course, he is happy to him and he begins to say, " I thought I would not see you here again, today."

"I'm always here and I have no other ways to get out of here", said Mr. Frog.

"You might have a chance to go someplace else if you want", said the duck.

"Yes, I heard that line before, but where the rest of your flock", asked Mr. Frog.

"Oh, they are all at the other lake and it is so beautiful site with plenty of food to catch. That lake has a huge body of water.

Also, there are many kinds of insects to catch food. It is very nice place to be there", said the duck.

"The lake, how far from here?", asked Mr. Frog.

"It is not too far from here", said the duck.

In this conversation between Mr. Frog and the young duck is kept on going and Mr. Frog wants to go to a new place because he has been here in this pond for all of his life. Even though Mr. Frog heard the young duck saying that the lake is not too far from here, he does not the ability to travel in a great distance on his own. Obviously, it is a great danger out there and Mr. Frog would not have a chance to be there alone traveling under the heat of the sun. Beside the extreme heat of the summer, there are many predictors rooming all over places and again Mr. frog will terribly be eaten alive by those wild and dangerous animals if he tries to go alone traveling in such as a great distance. Literally, there is no second chance if one little mistake is made.

Up high in the air, Gray tries to catch up with Spotty, but he was a little too late to pull himself out from water. By the time he was up in the air, Spotty was completely out of his sight. There is no way that he can catch up with Spotty. Gray does not want to be hurry because he knows exactly where Spotty is going to. Then, he decides to fly lower and keeps his eyes on the ground to see if he can find another pond. As he is in the air flying from a big cluster of wild bushes to the next, he always has eyes looked for a small spot of water where there are usually little fishes swimming in a shallow water because water gets dried very fast in the summer. Soon he comes over a big hill located behind thick bushes, there is something that he sees lying still on grass. He quickly turns around and flies back to the big hill.

This is moment of fear, Gray has his eyes focused on a wing lying still on the grass. This is something that he does not expect to see. On his way flying down to the ground, he is feeling nervous and very sick in his stomach. This is, of course, not easy to see one of his fellows getting killed. At the same time, he thinks of Spotty. Gray has lost a few good friends in a hunting season. He never gets over the fact that he and his friends, one day, flew home in the sunset and talked about where they wanted to go, next day, to search for food. All of sudden, the bullets flew through the chest and came out from the back. The three good friends of his dropped down to a swamp and Gray had to fly spiral down to the swamp. He pretended that he got hit. Soon he got low enough to the water, he flapped his wing and flew low behind thick bushes so that hunters would not see him. Then, he quickly flew up straight to sky. He continued flying high and went behind the clouds.

A silent moment on the ground, Gray looks around to see if anything strength is coming by. Then, he walks toward a wing which is moving by a gentle wind brushes on feathers. There is nothing that Gray can do, but to stand still staring at the wing. At least, he feels much better to know that Spotty is somewhere and he is safe. Does not know what to do, Gray walks around the wing in the grass and pecks the tips of green grass to eat. Then, he takes a few steps toward one more time and then runs his beak gently on the feathers for several times before he decides to turn around and flies away.

In the opened space above the earth, Gray flies as fast as he could so that he can catch up with Spotty at the pond where he met Mr. Frog. He knows the world better than Spotty does. Of course, he tries to tell Spotty not to wander around unfamiliar places because danger is always waiting to happen. Also, life is unfortunately at uncertainty. However, Gray often tries to tell Spotty about consequences that life will have to face and this can be absolutely hurtful or dead. Gray does not want to see another of his good fellow get shot down from the sky. He was absolutely terrified to witness his friends got shot down from the sky and he, himself, barely got away a live. This is a horrible experience that Gray does not want Spotty to face. It is about life and death situation and Gray knows that Spotty is young and could not handle this kind of matter. Sometimes, Gray feels frustrated because he tries so hard to guide young Spotty to see a reality of their own lives living and breathing in the world where their lives are not guaranteed for their safety in the future. But, young Spotty has not learned anything, just yet, about his own world in which he thinks that this is a peaceful world.

From the day he has learned how to fly, Spotty assumes that he knows just about anything around him. He only sees himself in good times with other friends and again he only sees the surface beauty of the world in which can probably hurt him deeply, sometimes in the future. Spotty is young and does not fully understand the real world and a sense of responsibility. Obviously, Spotty likes to have fun and goes along with the crowd. He just can't see how life getting through a tough reality in this world. In other words, it is very sad that a tragedy will occur and life will be lost because most of youngsters, like Spotty, do not look close enough to see what happening in surrounding area.

Back to Gray who is very much concerning about Spotty 's safety is trying to guide young Spotty facing the real world. In the future, he can learn how to handle his own situation in a bad time. Flying above tree tops, Gray can see the pond through the branches. Then, he flies circle the pond, not only trying to slow himself down, but also to see anything dangerous coming around the pond. Gray smoothly glides himself down toward water and sees Spotty talking with Mr. Frog. Of course, it is a big release and he knows for sure that Spotty is okay. He swims slowly toward both of them, Spotty and Mr. Frog. It is quite a surprise that Spotty sees Gray approaching him from behind. Then, Mr. Frog turns to Gray and says, " Hey, fellow and I thought you never come here again." Gray quickly turns to Mr. Frog and says, " Hi ! Mr. Frog. Yes, I still come here when I can." In his mind, Spotty think of a reason why Gray comes after him, or perhaps there is something wrong. He does not want to ask Gray why he is here. Spotty turns around and looks at Gray. " I'm glad to see you here", said Spotty.

Then, Mr. Frog tells the two young ducks that he needs to take a rest at noon time because he has a long conversation with Spotty for a while. At the moment, Mr. Frog is about to turn around and walks toward his place and Spotty tells Mr.

Frog that he will help him to a nice place. Mr. Frog looks at Spotty with hope of going to a new place and he says, " thank you." Now, it is quiet and the two young ducks are left alone in the pond. After Mr. Frog has left, the two young duck swim side by side to the in front where they can easily fly out.

It is about early in the afternoon and the sun is up in the blue skies and the heat from the sun is gradually getting warmer in the atmosphere. The wind seems to die down in hot days of summer. There are big and small birds in tall trees to cool themselves down and other animals find themselves staying in the shade of big trees while the extreme heat of the sun is blasting across the universe. At this time of the day, there are not many birds flying from trees to trees. For a nice spot up in the tree, there are squirrels sitting on a big tree limb chewing nuts. In the pond, the young duck have nothing to do and they do not want to stay in the pond for any longer. They need to fly back to their flock at another big pond. Gray takes the lead and he takes off from the pond. Then, Spotty begins his flying after Gray. Up high in the sky, the two of them fly side by side.

In the air flying back to their flock, they seem not to have anything to share with each other. So, it is a silent moment becoming a mutual feeling for one another. Gray does not want to mention anything about a dead wing that he found lying on the grass when he was on his way to find Spotty at the pond where Mr. Frog is living. If Gray tells Spotty about his frightening day in the past, he feels like he is reliving the old pain. he knew that Spotty would not care for what have happened. He was not there to witness what were the problems existed in the past.

Gray does not like reminding himself about a terrifying day coming home from a long day searching for food. In that particular day, his friends were unfortunately shot to death from the sky. Gray was in great fear for his own sake because he came very close to lose his life. From this bad experience in his life, Gray comes to think that peace seems to only exist in everyone's mind. Out there in the real world, killing is often taking place just about in any corner of isolation area in wetlands and in large forest. Gray knows some dangerous places since he has been around in this region. He tries to avoid flying across this region as much as he can because many lives have been lost from flying across this region. This is also the main reason that he tries often to tell Spotty to see the world from different ankles; not the beauty of it that makes him think that the world is at peace.

On the other hand, Spotty is very young and he is so immature. He does not realize why he is so safe for being in this crowd of his own flock. In the past, this flock lost its members, one by one, during hunting season. These wild ducks took a long time to learn how to recognize the routes and places to search for food. Spotty is a new member in the flock and he has not faced a life threatening, yet. Right now, he seems to be very quiet because he thinks of a way to help Mr. Frog to get to a new place. He does not want to ask Gray for his help and he just waits for the right time to ask him.

Up from the clear sky, they can see the pond and Gray and Spotty can't wait to go to the pond and catch something to eat. The good part is the sun is still shining and there are not many members of their flock in the pond. Most wild ducks spend for hours in deep water trying to catch small fishes to eat. Even though, it is very hot in the summer, but it is actually cold in the depth of water. For those ducks have been in the water for long time, they came out from the pond and stayed in a grassy field behind the hills to get warmed up from the sun. Since it is in the afternoon, these ducks are just lying around in the sun for a little while. Well, this is kind of short break and the ducks enjoy themselves in the heat before going back in the water to catch more fish.

Without no time to wast, Gray and Spotty come in the pond and go under the water to catch their meal. They begin to get busy under water and they try to catch as many fish as they can. Now and then, they come up the surface with fish in their beaks. They lift up their heads and shake their beaks from side to side so that the fish can easily go down their throats. Sometimes, they come to the surface without fish in their beaks. Actually, they come up to the surface to breath and to look around to see if anything stranger come by the pond. They stay floated in the surface of water for ten, or fifteen seconds and then they go back down to the depth of water again. The two young ducks continue chasing a school of fish in deep water for a while and they catch enough fish to eat. Then, the cold gets through their skin and they do not feel like to chase small fish anymore in the deep water. They both come up to the surface and swing to the shore. In the hot sun, they stand on the grass and shake the feathers.

Slowly but happily, they stroll toward their flock lying in the sun to get warm. A few of them stand up in the crowd when Gray and Spotty come to join the group. They stand up and talk to one another for a few minutes and then they all get back down to the ground lying on the grass. Now and then, a few of them in the group turn their bodies from side to side while they are comfortably resting in the heat.

Soon it is time to go back to the pond, the flock of wild ducks spreads out on the grassy field and they leisurely stroll back toward water. The ducks seem to be slow and lazy when they walk back to the pond. As soon as they get in the water, most of these wild duck get energized. They begin flapping their wings and quickly dip their heads in water. Some of them chase one another for a short while, just for fun. After a long break, they need to work together as a team to catch fish. this is the second half of the day and it is also last catch of the day, as well. They have to catch as many fishes as they can because they still have plenty of time to enjoy the day and catch more fish to eat. However, when the sun starts going down in the evening, they have to get ready to come back home.

As the day is still bright, the wild ducks come together and work their way in deep water to catch fish. They chase a school of fish. They peck small fish, one by one, and come up to the surface of water to catch their breathe. The ducks get back down to the deep water quickly so that they catch more fish to eat. At the same time, a school of fish seems to get confused and panic when a big flock of wild ducks come quickly charging at vulnerable little fish. Again, deep down in the bottom of this pond, little fishes try to swim away from hungry ducks. They attempt to get away from one duck and the others come right at them and scary little are quickly pecked by strong beaks and brought to surface, and finally little fishes are swallowed alive. Of course, some other ducks are much aggressively chasing little fishes because they are still hungry.

However, it looks very much peaceful on the surface of water. Everything else is normal. There are some colorful butterflies flying above the surface of water. They go from flowers to flowers as they wish. A few dragonflies stay still on the tip of tiny water plants which are being rocked back and forth by a blow of soft wind that comes across the grassy field and brushes over the pond. The birds are pleasantly chirping in the bushes and hopping from branches to branches. Some other big birds are up high in the sky searching for something else to eat.

At this huge pond, or big lake, the water is clear and it seems not get any lower in the summer. This huge pond is located in a landscape where there is not many big trees standing by, Also, there is not many bushes growing around the pond. There is a very huge field stretching surrounded the pond and from any direction, the pond can be well seen in a low flat land. It is more land and big space for big birds and other animals to roam by the pond.

In the early morning, the pond has its beauty embraced in a golden sunshine. There are beautiful flowers standing tall in the middle of the pond showing off the bright colors of white, yellow, red and pink in the sun. The cool breeze comes across the pond and gently rocks the flowers back and forth. Then, the crystal drops of morning dew begin slowly rolling down the curves and falling into the pond.

At this monstrous lake, there are different kinks of water plants growing in the pond which provides shelters to some small birds and insect. Underneath of these water plants, there are schools of fish often coming around to find something to eat from the roots of plants that float on the surface of water. Obviously, this lake becomes a feeding ground. From small insect to large birds, they all come here to catch their food and to take a rest in the middle of the day.

Unusual Travel

IT IS EXACTLY the same place, at the monstrous lake, where they were here yesterday. At this time, it is roughly about noon time. The flock of wild ducks takes an afternoon break in the sun. They are literally scattering all over the grassy field. Some of the ducks are lying flat on their bullies and stretching their soaked wings to dry in the heat. A few others are aimlessly walking around and pecking the tips of young grass. Most of them are comfortably ly- ing in the field after having enough to eat.

In the moment, Gray is quietly lying in the sun and he is just about to close his eyes. And here he is, Spotty approaches Gray lying comfortably on the grass. He thinks this should be the right time and he tries to ask Gray for a little help. This moment, he hopes that Gray would agree to help him. Spotty really needs Gray's help because he could not do this job alone. This was that Spotty has promised Mr. Frog to take him to a new pond. Therefore, Spotty puts himself in a bad position which he could not do it by himself. The trouble is that he makes himself look bad and he has no body else would come to help, but Gray. Again, the problem is that he seems not to think of what to say before he decides to do something. In this case, Spotty literally puts his foot in his own mouth.

As Spotty walks toward Gray, he is nervous, not because he is afraid of Gray might say something bad to him, but because he is nervous because Gray might say no to him. That means that Gray does not want to help and he does not want to get involved with whatever Spotty needs him to do.

In previous times, Spotty has tried to ask Gray for a favorite and Spotty got nothing from Gay, but No for an answer. Spotty did not really know what else he could do for Mr. Frog, but to spend time with him while he was trying hard to get help from Gray. This was not easy to depend on someone for assistance and Spotty did not want to give up on Mr. Frog. Some other times, he felt very bad when he was thinking that he could not help Mr. Frog. Somehow, this negative feeling has kept Spotty trying to get help.

Patiently, Spotty stands still before Gray and he waits for Gray to say something. Inside of him, Spotty wishfully hopes that Gray would change his mind and come to help him. In a second, Gray wonders why Spotty standing here and says nothing. While he is lying comfortably on the grass, Gray looks up to see what is wrong with Spotty. This is the first time and he, of course, has never seen Spotty acting calm and this quiet.

"What is wrong with you", asked Gray. Spotty still says nothing, but looking at gray.

"Can you hear me! I said what is wrong with you?", Gray repeated himself.

"I don't think I have somebody to talk to", said Spotty.

"What are you talking about?", asked Gray.

"That is my point and nobody wants to hear me", said Spotty.

"You have something else to tell me about", said Gray.

"That something else is my problem and that problem is that I want to help Mr. Frog to get to a new place", said Spotty.

A moment of silence, Gray slowly gets up and stands on his feet with his eyes staring at Spotty. Still, not a word is being said and Gray walks around pecks on a few tips of green grass. Silently, he thinks to himself that every creature has a set of skills to survive in this world. Fighting through bad weather and flying far across region after region to search for food are all parts of surviving in order to lead young generation to do the same thing. Obviously, danger comes in different forms and shapes trying to destroy other lives for pleasure and for food. Young generation does not know anything out there. Spotty is one of the young generation and he does not have a clue. Of course, Gray knows that it is worthless to tell Spotty about a productive life living in this flock.

For whatever the reason, Gray does not absolutely understand why Spotty wants to do something like that, helping Mr. Frog to get to a new pond. Gray decides to go along with Spotty's idea, but he knows that this could be much worst. So, he hopes for the best.

"I don't know how we can help Mr. Frog to get to a new place", said Gray.

"Yes, we can with your help", said Spotty. "We are flying in the air and Mr. Frog is not going to make it", said Gray.

"That is the reason I need you to help me take Mr. Frog to a new place", said Spotty.

"I don't have anything to make Mr. Frog can fly", said Gray.

"I think I have a plan to take Mr. Frog to a new place", said Spotty.

"I am not so sure about the plan you have. It's going to be a disaster", said Gray.

"Why you say that", said Spotty.

"You said that you want to help Mr. Frog, but I don't see anything that is possible to take Mr. Frog to a new place", said Gray.

"I have something at Mr. Frog's place that would help in a process of taking Mr. Frog to a new place. We have to go now and the day is still young", said Spotty. Don't want to waste any more time talking, they both take off and fly to Mr. Frog's place. However, Gray has a big question in his mind when he heard Spotty saying that he has something which can be used to help Mr. Frog to get to a new place. Gray wonders what is something that Spotty has and he has never seen what Spotty has in his possession. In second thought, Gray can feel deeply down in his guts that there is something going wrong, but he does not know exactly what will be taken place. Gray is not very pleased with Spotty 's plans and the idea of helping Mr. Frog to get to a new place.

Then, they both, Gray and Spotty, get to Mr. Frog and spotty is so happy to tell Mr. Frog a good news that he is going to a new place to day at this moment. Mr. Frog can't help himself and he is so happy when he heard the a good news. He has been waiting for this trip to a new place for along time. He is so excited and literally starts doing a little hopping around for enjoyment. On the other hand, Spotty is so glad to see Mr. Frog enjoying his moment. This is it, today is the day that Mr. Frog will go to a new place as Spotty has made a promise to help Mr. Frog moving.

However, Gray stands quietly by himself watching the two, Mr. Frog and Spotty, of them having a little fun for the moment. At the same time, Gray looks around the place and sees nothing that can be used to carry Mr. Frog to a new place. He does not know why Spotty is so happy about helping Mr,

Frog to get to a new pond. Nothing here can be used for any purpose, especially for the use to carry Mr. Frog to the new place. Now, Gray begins to fear for the unusual trip in the sky because Mr. Frog can't obviously fly. This is something that Gray has seen from the beginning which is not good. Spotty wants to do something that is not meant to be. For example, helping Mr. Frog to get to the new place is totally out of line. Spotty can't teach Mr. Frog how to fly.

Then, Gray turns around to see Mr. Frog and Spotty bragging about flying to the new place. The joy of going to the new place makes them forget of what to prepare for the trip. Gray knows that this trip is going to be a disaster and the two of them, Spotty and Mr. Frog, do not realize. For his prediction, Gray can visualize that the danger and there is someone going to be hurt, or could be killed because of carelessness and the lack of preparation for the trip. Gray needs to take a few steps toward Spotty and has to say something before someone will get hurt. Quietly, Gray comes to stand before Mr. Frog.

"Hello Mr. Frog, I can see you're very excited", said Gray.

"I'm so happy to go to the new place", said Mr. Frog.

"I'm glad that we can help you to another place, but excuse me for a second and I want to talk with Spotty", said Gray.

"Okay, go ahead. Let me get ready for the trip", said Mr. Frog.

Quickly, Gray turns around to see Spotty and asks him to step away from Mr. Frog for a second because he has something to discuss about this unusual journey. This is the first time that Gray gets himself involved with Spotty 's plan to get Mr. Frog to the new place. Obviously, there is something that Gray does not know and understand what and why Spotty wants to help Mr. Frog. It is very dangerous to take someone up high in the air. This kind of strange work has never done in the previous time because it could possibly cause someone's life. At the beginning of the trip, Gray has necessarily to go over with Spotty because he seems not to see the danger waiting to happen.

It is far enough from Mr. Frog and Spotty looks at Gray and asks him a question. Again, Spotty is acting with confidence and he thinks that there is nothing going wrong with this trip. Of course, this is not going to be okay with Gray about flying high for a long trip because Mr. Frog comes along with this trip. This is the time that Gray wants to know what exactly Spotty has prepared himself for this journey and also he wants to know what is an accommodation for Mr. Frog on this journey. Literally, this trip is not very safe to start with and Gray does not feel comfortable. He has to talk with Spotty.

"You ask me for my help for this trip, but I don't see anything getting prepared to take off", said Gray.

"Don't worry, I'll get this ready in a minute when Mr. Frog is ready", said Spotty.

"Get what ready, I don't see anything prepared in front of me", said Gray.

"Nothing much to prepare and the trip is not that far from here to the lake where our flock is resting in the afternoon on a grassy field", said Spotty.

"What!", Gray screams at Spotty and Mr.

Frog quickly starts staring at Gray.

"You know there is just a little thing to go wrong and someone will get killed on this unprepared trip", said Gray.

"I don't plan to kill anybody. I just want to help Mr. Frog", said Spotty.

"You just don't care and you do thing when you wanted to. You don't want to look into your work to make sure it is safe", said Gray.

"What is wrong with this trip that concerns you", said Spotty.

"Right, there is nothing wrong with this trip, but there is something wrong with your head that you can't see", said Gray.

"I don't understand why I always have a problem when I ask you for help. It seems like I'm the problem and it does not matter what I do and you just like it and you always a mistake in my work", said Spotty.

Then, Mr. Frog wonders why these just standing over there and they have been talking for a while. He decides to come closer to see what is really happening between the two of them. He walks slowly and quietly so that he would not want to disturb them. Mr. Frog stays calm and listens to the unpleasant tone of their conversation and he knows that they are getting upset of thing. He still does not understand what is the real problem between the two of them. There is something that he does not know that has caused the two of them to be upset. Later, he has a second thought that this is no good if the two of them keep going at each other with an unpleasant tone in this conversation. Mr. Frog moves closer to them and starts coughing loudly to clear his throat so that the two of them can see him standing by. Quickly, the two of them, Gray and Spotty, turn around to look at Mr. Frog with a surprise on their faces. Actually, they do not know for how long that Mr. Frog has been standing behind and listening to their conversation.

"Hay Mr. Frog", they both responded to Mr. Frog.

"Is everything okay?", asked Mr. Frog. "It is good to hear that and you two doing Okay", said Mr. Frog.

"Oh, we are doing great", said Spotty. "Are we still going to the new place today", asked Mr. Frog.

"Of course, we're going to the new place to day, but just give a minute to get ready", said Spotty.

Soon Mr. Frog walked to get himself ready for the trip, Gray asks Spotty for what is the thing that can be used to carry Mr. Frog to the new pond. Spotty takes a few steps away from Gray and pecks a stick which is about three feet long to show Gray that this is the thing would be used to carry Mr. Frog to the new pond.

Quietly, Gray just stands still with his eyes staring at the long stick and also staring at Spotty. This is exactly the problem that he has thought about Mr. Frog's safety. Absolutely, he knew this from the beginning and he just waited to see what Spotty can help Mr. Frog. Gray knew all along that Spotty wanted to Mr. Frog, but he does not know how to help. This preparation for the trip is clearly that Gray can visualize the trouble which is about to happen on the way to the new place. At the moment, Spotty just stands there before Gray with his mind wondering what is Gray really thinking about the trip because he has not heard Gray saying anything. So, Spotty just stays quiet.

"Tell me how you carry Mr. Frog with this stick", asked Gray.

"Well, you and I bite on each end of the stick and Mr. Frog hold onto the middle of the stick and we just take him to the new pond", said Spotty.

"I just can't believe you're doing like this. It is stupid. You and I would easily get Mr. Frog killed on his way to the new pond", said Gray.

"I will tell him to hold on tight to the stick while we're flying", said Spotty.

"Stop it! You know nothing about helping someone", said Gray.

This is no use to talk about the trip, or to talk about Spotty. It does not matter at this point because Spotty has already told Mr. Frog that he is going to the new place. Also, the time of the day is in a late afternoon and the trip is about to get ready in any minute. Gray literally feels bad, not only about the unsafe trip, but also about himself being here and could not do anything to help. All he needs is that Mr. Frog wants to go away from this pond as soon as he can and at the same time Spotty puts himself in a dangerous position which he does not realize how bad the trouble he is in. He only see one thing that makes him look good is to help Mr.

Frog to another place. If Gray stepped in and stopped the trip, he would be exactly a bad character. Obviously, he is here to help, not to do anything.

Now, it is the time to begin the unusual trip to the pond. Mr. Frog is so delighted for having friends to help when he really needs assistance. Then, Spotty carry a long stick in his beak to the opened space. He quickly gives Mr. Frog the instruction about the trip and tell Mr. Frog how to be strong and be patient because this is going to be a difficult journey that Mr. Frog never has in his life. On the other hand, Gray stands on the other side quietly watching Spotty stepping back and forth over the stick. At the moment, Spotty acts like he knows just about anything and Mr. Frog stays quiet and pays attention to what spotty is trying to say. Because of his strong desire to leave his old place for good, Mr. Frog would do exactly what has said. In the back of his mind, Gray just thinks to himself. This is a blind leading the way. Gray does not want to say anything against the plan that Spotty has in mind because he knows that they will not listen, or believe what he has to say. From the beginning, Gray has told Spotty not to get involved with this kind of problem and he did not listen to Gray's idea. However, Spotty did not care what Gray has said to him. Gray knows that there is no use to say about this trip. Of course, he does not feel comfortable about this journey.

Trouble In The Air

JUST A FEW minutes before takeoff, Mr. Frog follows the instruction which Spotty has explained. He feels good about it. He just wants to get out of here and this is the very first time that Mr. Frog has a chance to travel above the earth. He wants to go out to see the world. Spotty is very happy for Mr. Frog that he can possibly help. Once again, Gray stands quietly with a little smile on face to show that he is happy for Mr. Frog, but deep down his guts; he is feeling sick. Gray knows that up in the sky is life and death that Mr. Frog has to face his own fear.

After a moment of celebration, the three of them line up as they have planned. Mr. Frog stays in the middle having his front legs grabbed the stick tightly. Both, Gray and Spotty bite on each end of the stick. Then, the countdown begins and Mr. Frog gets himself ready. Without any question about the trip, the two young ducks pull Mr. Frog up in the air. For the first glance at the world from the above, it looks so beautiful. The huge body of land is wildly stretching far out of sight. Streets are literally curved like little snake crawling on top of each other. On a street, there are some people walking down the the street and they look very small. There are many running down the roads and they look just like ants crawling in lines.

Up in the sky, Mr. Frog is amazed by the beauty of the world which has never seen in his life. He only uses to swamp where he began his early life living under water and hopping along the shore of the pond to search insect to eat. He is very glad deciding to move from his old place to search for a better of way of living. He can see the world offers more opportunity to all living creature on earth to live with their own skills to manage difficulty in life. Mr. Frog hopes that he would get a better chance in the new place than his old swamp. While he is holding onto the stick, Mr. Frog keeps open and observes a large grassy and long rolls of trees on the ground.

However, on his unusual trip to the new place, Mr. Frog does not feel comfortably to be this high, but it is too late to turn around. For somehow, He sees his own reality and he starts concerning about his life. Up in the air about fifteen minutes, Mr. Frog has his second thought drifted circle in the back of his mind about death. This does not look easy like he was thinking when he was on the ground. Flying high above the earth, he starts having a feeling of nervousness to face own death. For that matter, he could fall to his death from the sky. For his sake, Mr. Frog tries to hold onto the stick for his dear life, his arms, or front legs begin gradually to feel pain from hanging to the stick and his body continues to swing back and forth in the wind. Mr. Frog is literally talking and screaming in fear for his life. At this moment, he thinks that he might not make to the new place alive.

At the same time, the two ducks hear Mr. Frog screaming, but they could not do any- thing to accommodate him on the flight. Obviously, they can not talk to one another because they carry the stick in their beaks. If they were talking to one another, the stick will come loose and Mr. Frog will fall to his death. Exactly, this is not an easy job to do by having Mr. Frog held onto the stick. They both try to keep the long stick stable so that it would be easy for Mr. Frog to hold onto. However, this is not a custom that Mr. Frog gets use to; flying high in the air is not meant for any Frog to get this high above the ground. Mr. Frog is scared to death and he can feel pain in his arms, or front legs for holding onto the stick for this long. In this case, he has no other options to take care himself on this flight. He has to do, holding on to his dear life.

Up in the sky, Gray knows what is happening, but he just can't do anything. When he feels a strong wind rushing against his body, he bites hard on the stick and pulls the stick hard to go down in oder to avoid the strong wind blowing against them. At the same time, Spotty does not understand why Gray keeps pulling the stick up and down. He wants to talk to Gray, but he can't. This is not the time to have a conversation. He has to bites hard on the stick and keeps flying. Also, Mr. Frog keeps yelling at the two ducks why they have to do that, pulling the stick down. Every time the stick is pulled down fast without warning, Mr. Frog feels a huge hole in his stomach and it scares him to death. Whatever the decision to go with his ideas, Gray knows that it is not going to be easy for Mr. Frog because Mr. Frog never gets himself up that high above the ground and secondly he has never been flying in the air.

For the time being, Gray needs to speed up because he can see that Mr. Frog having a difficulty to keep himself holding on to the stick. He looks very frightening with his body swinging in a strong flow of the wind. He just feels bad for Mr. Frog has to come this way. Other times, he feels frustrated that Spotty is not listening to him and this is a miserable trip for everyone. At the moment, Gray does not feel comfortable with a stick in his beak and he begins to feel pain in his lower jar from biting hard on the stick. Now, he has come for this far on the trip and he has to be patient for a little longer until he well reaches Mr. Frog's new place.

This trip is more difficult than everyone expects. Flying high against the strong flow of the wind in the opened space above the earth is a great challenge. If Mr. Frog knew that it is very risky to come on this journey, he would not have a desire to give up his old place. Now, he has to put up with this kind of traveling which he is scared for his life. He does not know where is his new place located. All he wants was to come along with these two young ducks and they take him to the new pond. Certainly, he does not know how much longer he can hold on to the wooden stick because he is getting tired and his front legs are in pain. And also his skin gets dried in the wind blowing against his body.

All of sudden, his body feels numb because his upper is in pain for long time. Of course, a minute after minute, his body just gives way and he, himself, seems to fall asleep in the cold wind blowing against his face. Mr. Frog does not realize that he just let go the stick. He is out and knows nothing at the moment. His body flips upside down many times in the air. Quickly, the two young ducks let go the stick and they fly fast downward to see what is happing to Mr. Frog. None of them know what has happened to Mr. Frog and it is a frightening surprise to see Mr. Frog floating in the air fast toward the ground. They literally try to scream at the top of their lungs and Mr. Frog is still out in an unconsciousness. Mr. Frog continues to fall fast and these is nothing that the two ducks can do to help, but to watch Mr. Frog falling with their heart beating in fear.

From the sky, Mr. Frog's body plunges through thin air and flips upside down in mid air. That is lucky and his body falls in a pond which is not the one that the two young want to take him to. Mr. Frog is not awake at all when his body hits the water. He just sink into water. Then, the two ducks come in the pond and search for Mr. Frog. They swim all over the pond and call out for him to come out, but there is nothing happening, not even Mr. Frog comes out to the surface of water. After that, they go deep in the water to look for Mr. Frog at the bottom of the pond. They hope to find him somewhere in the bottom of the pond. Gray and Spotty search for Mr. Frog everywhere in the pond, from the surface of the water and deep down to the bottom of the pond. They still can't find Mr. Frog anywhere. They begin to feel frustrated and very sad. They clearly saw Mr. Frog's body falling in the pond and they can't find him anywhere in the pond.

Obviously, it is very late in the evening and the sun is about to sink in the West. Right now, they have to put off the search and they need to go back to their flock while it is still bright in the day light. They take off from the pond and fly backup to the sky. Of course, they are hungry and emotionally sad to lose Mr. Frog. From this accident, Gray takes it hard on himself because he knew from the beginning that this trip was not going to make it and somebody would get hurt in the process of moving from one place to another. He even took time to explain Spotty why this trip was not good. However, Gray still got himself involved in this disastrous journey. He knows he should have stopped the trip, but he did not. Instead, he went along and took control of it. That was the reason that hurts him badly inside. Flying back home, Gray does not talk at all and silence seems to ease his emotional pain.

Deep in a summer night, it is still warm and the wind is barely blowing. Everything else is standing still in a wall of darkness. Every duck in the flock is peacefully sleeping, Gray was still awake thinking about the accident which has caused Mr. Frog's life. He is quietly lying in the sand and looking into the darkness of the night. In his mind, he keeps thinking about Mr. Frog and what has happened to him and is he okay? And then, Spotty comes and he just wants to talk with Gray.

The two ducks begin to talk about stories back in the past. Under the cool blow of the wind in the middle of the night, they share the story of the time when they were young and learn how to walk. At some parts of their, they are laughing for the moment when they remember the funny things they did. Laugh after laugh, they both, Gray and

Spotty feel good about themselves and they seem to forget problems. Gray feels happy that he can talk to Spotty and he listens to him. At least, they are both on the page and try to understand each other.

In the conversation, Spotty asks Gray why he always follows him and lets him know a warning sign of danger. It is a moment of silence and Gray turns around to look at Spotty. Then, Gray thinks to himself that it is the perfect time that Spotty should know.

"I thought you never ask why I always with you", said Gray.

"Yes, no matter where I am at, you are always there beside me", said Spotty.

"I think you are big enough to understand what I'm about to tell you", said Gray.

"Oh! You have another hilarious story to tell me", said Spotty.

"It's funny. I'm always with you because I was told to do that. I have to keep my words and that is my promise to them", said Gray.

"I'm glad that you want to know whom I have made a promise to and I will tell you exactly what was happening", said Gray.

"I'm ready and tell me a story", said Spotty.

The night is quiet and the cool wind begins to brush through bushes and to keep the atmosphere cool at night. The two ducks are comfortably lying in soft sand and enjoy the night. Spotty waits patiently to hear the story and Gray says, "here the beginning of the story". It was the time when you, Spotty, was very little and you could not fly and your grandparents were too old to fly. Your parents had often to leave you with your grandparents when they went out to search for food. Back then, I was big enough to fly and I tried to keep up with your parents flying in the sky. They knew a lot of safe places to go and brought home the food for you and your grandparents. They worked very hard to feed you and your grandparents and I never heard a complain from them. They were happy to bring home food so that you and your grandparents could have something to eat each day.

For over the years, I have learned a lot from them about where I should go and what I should look out for myself and others. Your father did not talk much, not because he did not like to talk, but because he had a lot in his mind about family. In the hot summer time, most ponds were dried and the bottom of the pond became empty, not even a drop of water in the pond. Every little living creature in the pond died by the heat of the sun. Now, your parents had to fly much and much further to search for food. The entire flock followed your father to look for food because they knew that your father knew safe places to find food to eat and nobody got killed on the way out to look for food, or on the way to come home. Of course, your father was a leader of the flock. He had a huge responsibility on his shoulders.

Deeper and deeper into his family story, Spotty does not make a sound. He wants to know who are his parents and where are they, now. He is wondering why nobody tell him anything about his parents and also why Gray seems to know a lot about his parents. Spotty has been waiting for a long time to hear about his family and he wants to search for them. He thinks this is the beginning where he should find his parents. Then, he asks Gray," You know where are my parents". Gray looks at Spotty and says, "I will tell in a minute". Spotty stays quiet and turn his beak to peck on his feather on the right wing.

So, Gray continues telling the story of Spotty 's family. As Gray is saying that it was a little late in the morning and it was a long way to get there. Your father decided to take a short cut flying over the village and every body else agreed with your father's decision. At the same morning, you were staying with your grandparents when your parents and the flock went out to find food. On that bright morning, the entire flock flew lower above the villages and farms. The flock continued flying toward forest and came over a swamp, but the flock did not stop there because there was nothing to catch in a shallow water. This long trip to search for food, nobody expected anything, but to find more food to feed youngsters and also to feed themselves. This was just a normal day flying in a crowd, like any other flock flew lower to find food.

However, that was the worst day I have ever faced in my life. Soon the entire flock flew over a second swamp where there were thick bushes surrounded that huge pond. Also, there were many tall trees with a lot of leaves in the trees. Obviously, nobody saw anything on the ground, but the top of big trees. Then, the flock came just a little over the swamp and the loud sound, bang, bang, bang and bang came from nowhere. There were more than a few of dropped down to the swamp. Your father got hit first and other three behind him got hit as well. After that, four more got hit and they were all killed before they dropped in the swamp. For the last two shot, there were two more hit and fell in the water. One of the last two were hit was your mother. She got hit badly on her right wing. Quickly, I went down to the swamp where your mother was lying. I tried my best to encourage her to get up and fly away.

Unfortunately, there was no use. She had broken bone and a big cut on the side of her body. She struggled very hard with one wing in the water. She was in a severe pain and her feathers were badly soaked with water and she was literally very exhausted. She breathed so fast with her eyes staring at me and I was scared. Obviously, she knew that she was not going to make it. Then, she said this, "Whatever happens to me, I want you to look after Spotty for me. I have nobody else to tell this, but you. This is the end of me, my life. I am only whom Spotty would call mommy, but he never knows and sees me well enough to recognize that I am his mother who would no longer exist in his life time. He is so little, just a baby. Now, I feel okay even though I have to bear the pain. I know Spotty in good hands and I hope you will not let down. I am ready for whatever I have to go through from here and I accept it," "You can count on me and I will take good care of Spotty", I said to your mother. Then, I had to fly away because two big dogs came in the swamp. That was a horrible morning and I never forget that day. That was a promise I have made to your mother that I would take good care of you after she was gone. Then, it was probably about three weeks later and I found your both grandparents lying dead. I did not have a clue why they both were dead. The only way that

I can think of was that they were very old, or perhaps they were worrying too much about their children being shot to death and they got severely ill and died. It was not easy for me from time to time when I had to stay with you. I could not leave you alone and flew away to search for food. I had to eat whatever I could and waited for the day you could fly on your own. I felt it took me forever to see you flying.

For a while, Gray does not hear Spotty saying anything and he turns around to look at him. He sees Spotty has his beak dropped to the ground. "Are you sleeping?", asked Gray. And Spotty said, "No, I can hear you clearly telling me the tragedy taken place in my family." And then, Gray said, "I'm sorry to tell you all of this sad story taken place in your family, But I have to let you know what has happened to your parents and grand- parents. I've waited for this long to tell you and it is not easy for me to go back and talk about this tragedy. I was there and I've seen it all. It was horrible. I'm sorry that you have to hear something like this about your family. Go to get some sleep and we have to find Mr. Frog tomorrow."

Deeper in a quiet night, the wind starts blowing strong cool air in the dark and tiny branches begin to rock back and forth and tall grass is being swayed from side to side under the blow of the wind. For Spotty, this is a difficult night to sleep in even though the cool breeze starts to blow across the atmosphere. Spotty has been quiet for entire night since he listens to what Gray tells him about his family. At night sleeping, he often changes his body from side to side. He seems to stay calm and relaxed, but inside of him, and he is emotionally hurt. For all his life, he hopes to meet his parents and thinks to begin his life with parents, just like other families. Unfortunately, it does not turn out to be as good as he expects. With high hope to meet his parents, he just can't accept the fact that this accident could happen to his parents. Of course, Spotty finds it very hard to night to believe that his parents were killed when he was a little.

By the time Spotty went to sleep, it was very late and when he woke up the morning, everybody was gone to search for food. Gray is walking by the pond and he pecks on the tips of young grass to eat. Also, he waits for Spotty to get up. When Spotty is about to take off, Gray yells out loud at him to come by the pond. Then, Spotty walks toward Gray and he is wondering why Gray wanders around the pond in the morning.

"What are you doing here by the pond?", asked Spotty.

"Come with me and I have something to show you", said Gray.

"I can't wait to see what is out there", said Spotty.

"I think this is important and you need to know", said Gray.

"Is there something else that I don't know", said Spotty.

"Yes, you were too little to remember them", said Gray.

"What are you talking about THEM", asked Spotty.

"You will see who I'm talking about", said Gray.

The two of them walk by the bushes to other side of the pond where Gray needs to show Spotty. He tries to keep up with Gray to the place where he wants to see what Gray wants to know about. Sooner they both get to the site, they just calmly stand still for the moment looking down to the ground without a word and Gray takes a few more steps closer to the spot on the ground. Spotty starts walking a few steps forward with Gray. "This is the spot you want me to come and see something", said Spotty.

"Yes, this is the spot and I want you to look at those feathers", said Gray.

"Yes, I see them and they are buried half in the ground", said Spotty.

"This is the spot where I found your grandparents lying dead in the ground and

I did not know why they came to die after a few weeks your parents were killed", said Gray.

Gray glances at Spotty standing quietly and takes a few backward. He leaves Spotty alone for the moment. He knows this is not easy for Spotty to go through his family tragedy. Spotty is the only one in the family who is still surviving and the rest of his family were killed on the way to search for food and his grandparents were badly sick and died from natural causes. Then, Spotty turns around and walks toward Gray and he says nothing. It is too much sorrow for him to bear and silence is an easy way for him to focus on his life and to do what best for himself. Literally, he has a lot to learn, not just a way to search for food, but also a way to understand the situation of reality. In general, life is not always in a safe side.

For a while, they spend enough time at the site where his grandparents were lying dead in the ground, they decide to fly after the flock and to find something to eat. On the way to be with the flock, they do not talk to one another, not because they hate each other, but because of the sadness in the family makes them stay quiet and have no desire to talk. They keep flying to the pond where they catch some fish to eat because they did not eat much yesterday. They were busy to search for Mr. Frog and even now, they do not know where exactly Mr. frog is. The way they observed, they do not think that Mr. Frog would not make it because he felt too far from the sky. It is hard to say that Mr. Frog is still a live even though he luckily felt into a pond. The fall, it is too far down from the sky. They both have to spend one more evening to look for Mr. Frog because they do not want to walk away without knowing what has happened to him after he felt in the water.

There is something that Gray has noticed in a very short time. He sees that Spotty has slightly grown, not the size of his young body, but his maturity has well grown to be an adult. Gray is glad to see Spotty has changed in his good behavior and he seems to listen more than doing thing without thinking. This is exactly the way that Gray really wants Spotty walk on for his life and for his own safety. Gray, himself, has been through many bad experiences in his life and he has been scared to death that he would not make out alive. He does not want Spotty to go through what he has been through because life could cut short. As long as Gray is still around, he would guide Spotty along the way so that he can learn more about life and reality in this trouble world.

After a short flight, Gray and Spotty reach the pond where the entire flock is busy chasing and catching fish in the bottom of the pond. The two of them do not want to waste any more time and they begin going down to the bottom of the pond and try to catch whatever they can eat. Right here at the pond, they have to spend long hours in the water to catch fish. If they are lucky, they can catch more fish in a couple of hours. Then, they can come up and stay warmer in the sun. Gray and Spotty still have plenty of time to catch fish to eat.

In the pond, there are a few ducks popping up the surface to catch their breath and also to look around for danger. There ducks seem to have a few of them taken turn to come up to the surface to look out for each other while the others are busy in the bottom of the pond. This is a better way that this flock can stay survived year after year in a way they stay together and look out for one another, just like Gray takes enormous time to look after Spotty when his parents were killed in a hunting season. For long hours, this flock of wild ducks spend their time in the water to catch their food. Sometimes, they fly back home with empty stomach because they have to avoid danger and other times, they can't find a good pond in the hot summer. Because of hunger, there wild ducks are patient and they keep trying to search for food by flying to different regions where they hope to find good ponds.

Of course, it is much late in the afternoon and those ducks come up to the surface and they swim back to the shore. They walk out from the water and come to lie down in the grassy field. Some of them stretch their wings and flap them very hard to shake of the water from their feathers. Most of them are lying down in the sun quietly to get warm up. In the heat of the sun, most small birds are staying in the cool shade of thick bushes and tall trees and also there are not many big birds flying around in the afternoon. While the wild ducks are comfortably lying in the grass, a big push of the cool wind comes strongly across the field. There are some small branches rocking back and forth and leaves are wildly rattling in the trees as the wind blows by. Since there is no duck in the pond, fish comes up to the surface to catch a quick breath of fresh air and goes back in deep water. This is the only chance that fish can come up to the surface to breathe some fresh air when the wild ducks are lazily lying in the sun. Right now, these ducks still enjoy the sun and they do not want to go back in water, any time soon.

It has been an hour that these ducks are so comfortably lying in the sun and most of them are still lying on the grass with their turning around to see if anyone of them goes back in the water. There are some big ducks walking around with their flapping. Then, the others get up and chase one another all over the field. Quickly, all of them get to stand on their and make loud noises before they get back in the pond. This is the second round of the day to catch more fish to eat before they hit back home. In other words, these wild ducks spend their time here by the pond all day looking for something to eat. Home is a safe place where they can come to sleep at night. In day time, they have to go places to find food and it does not matter how far they have to go, food is very important source for their lives. If a couple is having a baby, a partner has to fly in a great distance at least six times a day in order to provide enough food for his partner and the baby. This is a kind of a job that a good partner has to sacrifice his leisure times and sometimes life could be lost because of a heavy obligation to feed the family. This is just like Spotty 's family. His parents were killed on the way to search for food.

Once again, this is the time for the second round of the day to catch something to eat before it is time flying back home. The entire flock starts walking toward the pond, but Gray and Spotty do not want to return to the pond. They have to look for Mr. Frog. For the second round of the day, they take off and fly to another pond where Mr. Frog has felt in the water and disappeared. They do not think in this case that Mr. Frog would be alive because he was falling fast down toward the earth. He felt fast and hard in the water. They have to come here one more time to look for him. If they can't find him in the pond, they would know that he did not make it.

When Gray and Spotty arrive at the pond, they stand on the shore looking across a huge body of water. They do not even know where to start looking and it is very quiet in the pond. The sun is shining bright in the afternoon. Along the shore, there are many tiny insect flying above the grass in shallow water. Also, there are many yellow butterflies flying from flowers to flowers and a few dragonflies stand still on the tips of dead branches which lean over the water. Again, it is quiet enough that fish comes up to the surface to catch a quick breath of fresh air and go back down to deep water.

Then, Gray starts slowly walking in shallow water and swimming with his eyes looking along the shore line. Spotty comes after Gray and he dips his beak in water and he drinks a little bit of it. He gets himself floated behind Gray with his eyes looking around to see if he can spot Mr. Frog. From one side of the pond to another, they both well search for Mr. Frog in every corner of the pond and along the shore line. Still, they can't spot his body. It has been two hours in this pond and they try hard with their best to locate Mr. Frog's body. Unfortunately, they find nothing. They do not know where else that they can go to look for his body and this is the pond that they saw Mr. Frog 's body in this big pond. The two of them, Gray and Spotty, look at each other in the face with a surprise. They just can't believe that Mr. Frog's body has disappeared for good. Now, they have nothing else to do in this pond, but to fly away from here.

They both come up to shore and stand in the sun for a short break and then fly back to their flock. The searching for Mr. Frog's body is over. They stand quietly on the shore with their eyes looking from one spot to another. While they are quietly standing on the shore, fish comes up quickly to the surface again to catch a breath of fresh air. As they continue looking into the pond, they see fish coming up to the surface here and there. Instead of flying back to join their flock, they decide to go back in the pond and catch some fishes to eat before they hit back home. In the bottom of the pond, they chase after a school of fish. Now and then, they come up to the surface of water with fish lying in their beaks. Soon they swallow the fish, they get back down to deep water and do the same thing, chasing a school of fish.

It is probably about an hour and they both enjoy catching fish in the bottom of the pond. Obviously, they do not expect any thing else, but to have plenty of food to eat before going back home. As usual, they go down to deep water and come up with fish in their beaks. They are both floating in the surface of water for a minute or two and watching around to see if any thing strange coming around. Then, they are about to go back down to the bottom of the pond, a voice comes from the other side of the big pond and says, " You two eat all my fish." They clearly heard the voice, but they can't see who is saying that. After that, they hear a sound like a rock being thrown in the water and they keep looking around and see nothing. So, here he is popping out from water, Mr. Frog. They both, Gray and Spotty, scream for joy, "You are alive!" The three of them are so happy to see each other again.

The moment of joy, the three of them begin talking about the trip and the fall that Mr. Frog could easily lose his life. They keep talking for hour and now it is time for Gray and spotty to go back home. On the way going back home, they both feel good and happy to see Mr. Frog doing okay after a long fall from the sky. However, Gray forgets to look where he is going. He actually flies over the hunting ground and he is in the middle of hunting zone. By the time he realizes that, it is too late to do any thing. He can't turn around since he and Spotty come this far. To go forward, they will be shot to death. This is the place where Spotty 's parents were shot to death when they were on their way to look for food. Gray begins to feel cold running through his body. At this moment, Spotty knows nothing and he does not have a clue. He just stays beside Gray flying back home. Gray does not have time to explain this thing to Spotty, not even a second.

Momentarily, Gray realizes that his life has come to an end. Quickly, Gray has to take action even though he know that he is not going to make out from this swamp alive. He begins to push

Spotty hard to get out of way. "What are you doing", Spotty is screaming at Gray. Bang, Bang, Bang... Gray gets hit in the chest and the bullet comes through his lower back. Gray takes a quick look at Spotty and then he is gone. Quickly, Spotty turns to look at Gray and he sees him falling downward. Spotty continues to scream for Gray to fly upward, but he is gone before he hits the ground. Spotty quickly flies upward and disappears behind the clouds.